PHOTOGRAPHIC HIGHLIGHTS OF

The Yorkshire Dales

BRADWELL
BOOKS

ABOUT

THE YORKSHIRE DALES

The Yorkshire Dales is an upland area of northern England, mostly falling within the Yorkshire Dales National Park which was designated in 1954. It is a collection of glacial river valleys and hills rising west of the Vale of York and extending to the Pennines, taking in some astonishing scenery along the way.

Most of the dales are named for the river which runs through them – Swaledale, Wharfedale, Malhamdale – and the area is criss-crossed by several long-distance walking and cycling routes. With rolling green hills, drystone walls, dramatic cliffs, tumbling waterfalls and plunging caves, the Yorkshire Dales is one of the most beautiful areas in England.

ANDREW

has worked as a graphic designer in advertising for over thirty years. His patience and attention to detail is reflected in the quality of his landscape photography. When he met Sue in 1996 they realised they shared a love of the countryside, and since then they have spent many weekends exploring the trails and remote areas of Britain. In addition to photography Andy is also a keen badminton player, an

accomplished cook (if it means using a wok) and has a passion for all things science fiction.

Equipment used:
Camera: *Canon 7D*
Lens: *Canon EF 17-40mm f/4L Ultra Wide Angle*
Processing: *Apple iMac 27" 2.9 GHz quad-core, running Photoshop CS6*

SUSAN

is a hairdresser with two grown children, Nicola and Simon. Her enthusiasm for photography began in 2001 when she acquired a small film camera, and in 2006 she progressed to digital imagery. She has absorbed many of Andy's photographic tips and skills, and there is now a friendly rivalry over who can get the best shots! She and Andy are able to hike most weekends, and she ensures she is fit enough for all the

walking by taking regular Pilates classes in her free time.

Equipment used:
Camera: *Canon 20D*
Lens: *Canon EF-S 18-55mm f/3.5-f/5.6*

PHOTOGRAPHIC HIGHLIGHTS OF

The Yorkshire Dales

A BOOK BY
ANDREW & SUSAN CAFFREY

BRADWELL
BOOKS

Published by Bradwell Books
9 Orgreave Close Sheffield S13 9NP
Email: books@bradwellbooks.co.uk
©Andrew & Susan Caffrey 2013

British Library Cataloguing in Publication Data:
a catalogue record for this book is available from
the British Library.

1st Edition

Hardback
ISBN: 9781902674919

Paperback
ISBN: 9781902674926

Print: BAYKO MATBAA Istanbul Turkey

Copywriting by: Louise Maskill
Design by: Andrew Caffrey

CONTENTS

INTRODUCTION

Welcome to our second book of photographic highlights. We began this series with the Peak District; we are lucky enough to live close to this stunning area of natural beauty, and walking here was the start of our interest in hiking and landscape photography.

We first discovered the Yorkshire Dales in 1999, and we were instantly captivated by the diverse scenery – the beautiful tumbling rivers and stunning waterfalls, the soft, gentle dales with their scatterings of barns and drystone walls, and the wild crags and ridges with their limestone pavements and dramatic cliffsides.

Capturing some of these images has been a test of endurance and patience. We have often waited for hours for the weather to change, and we have returned to the same places year after year to get that perfect shot of a particular landscape. We have walked through this astonishing landscape time and again, capturing the views that we love for you to enjoy in this book. Duly inspired, we hope that we might encourage you to visit some of the places you have seen on these pages.

UPPER WENSLEYDALE

A WALK AROUND HAWES AND APPERSETT

Wensleydale is one of the few dales not named after its river (the Ure), but the old name of Yoredale can still be found on some maps. Upper Wensleydale is famous for Hardraw Force, the highest unbroken waterfall in England, as well as the production of Wensleydale cheese in the village of Hawes, at the head of the valley.

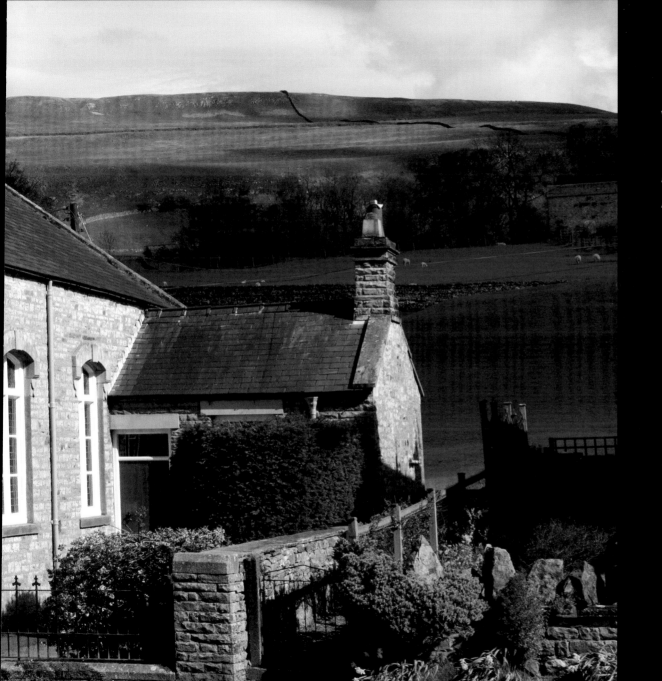

LOWER WENSLEYDALE

AROUND WEST BURTON, AYSGARTH AND HORSEHOUSE

The rich, fertile valley downstream of the thriving market town of Leyburn is home to the dairy herds which supply the Wensleydale creamery at Hawes. The River Ure tumbles down the limestone steps of Aysgarth Falls, and the area is rich in medieval history with castles at Middleham and Castle Bolton and the twelfth century abbey at Jervaulx.

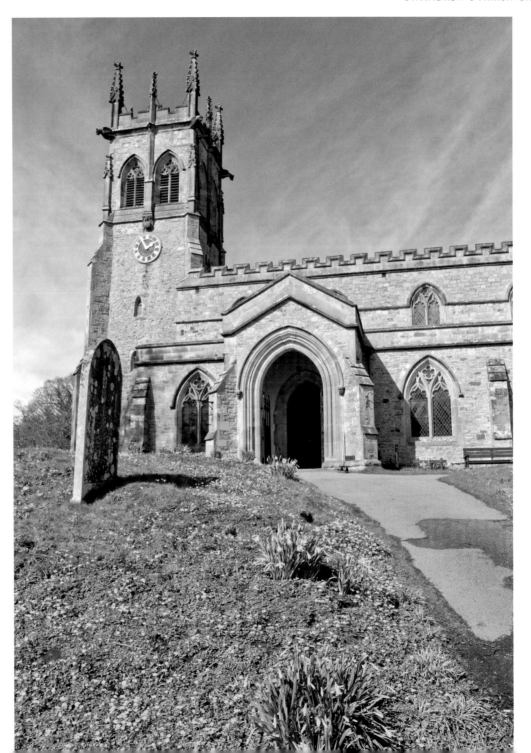

MALHAMDALE

THE LIMESTONE CLIFFS AND PAVEMENTS OF MALHAM COVE

Malham lies at the upper end of the valley of the River Aire, surrounded by classic limestone scenery of cliffs, crags and scars. Malham Cove, above the village, is a stunning natural limestone amphitheatre while the deep gorge of Gordale Scar was formed when a huge cave system collapsed. The beautiful Malham Tarn is the highest freshwater lake in the country.

RIBBLESDALE

SOUTH FROM RIBBLEHEAD BETWEEN INGLEBOROUGH AND PEN-Y-GHENT

The iconic Ribblehead viaduct, on the Settle-to-Carlisle railway, stands at the top of Ribblesdale. From its source in the moorland at Ribblehead the Ribble cuts between two of the Dales' Three Peaks running through Selside and Horton in Ribblesdale and then on past Settle and out into the gentler countryside of the Ribble Valley.

SWALEDALE

REMOTE AND UNSPOILT - GUNNERSIDE, KELD AND EAST GILL FORCE

Swaledale is one of the northernmost dales in th
National Park, running from the high moors on
the border with Cumbria to the medieval town
of Richmond. The steep valley sides and rough
moorland skyline contrast with waterfalls, sheep
farms and wildflower meadows. The dale also ha
a rich industrial heritage, with ruined lead mines
crumbling into the landscape.

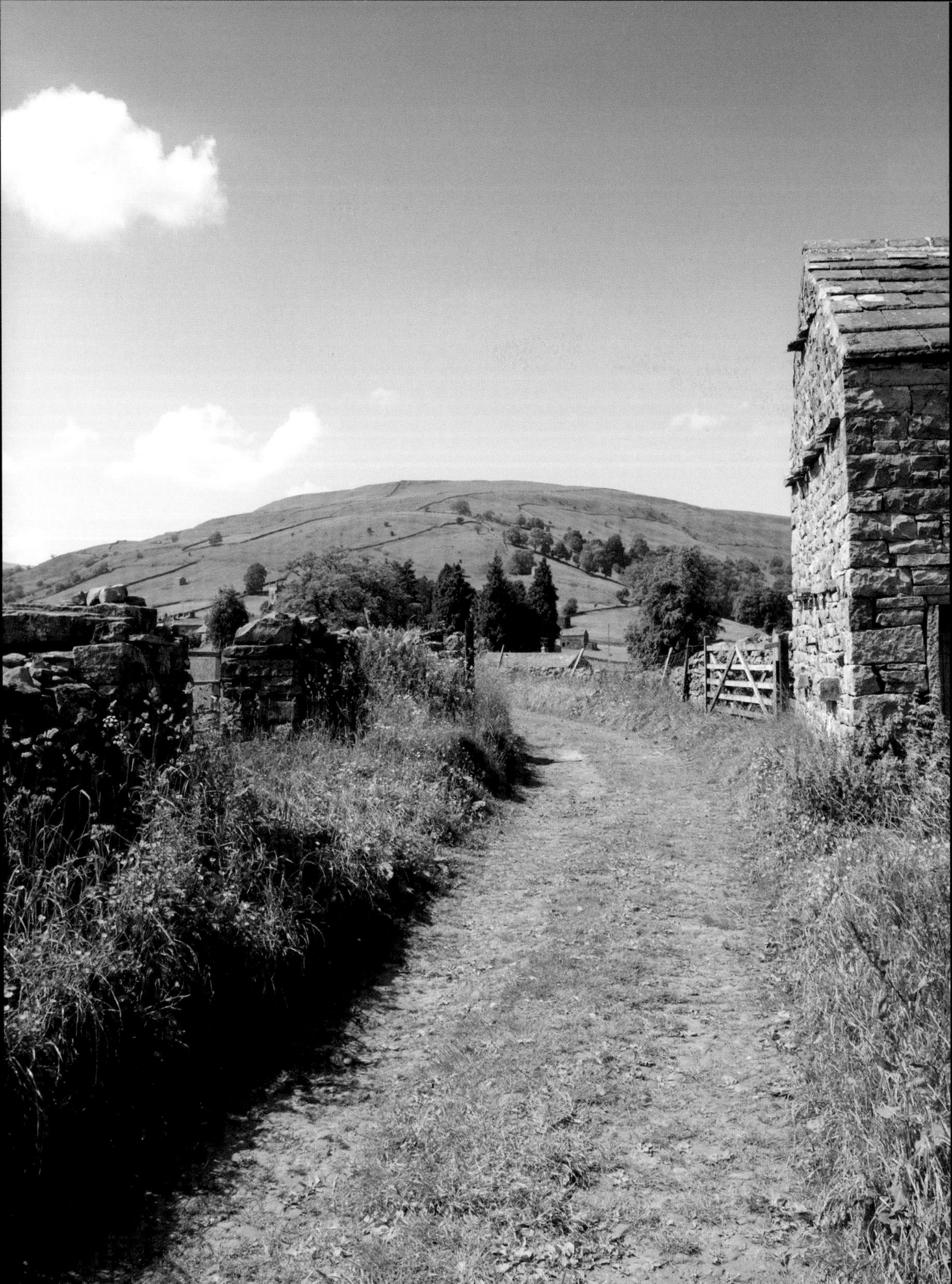

UPPER WHARFEDALE

LIMESTONE VILLAGES AND THE FORBIDDING OVERHANG OF KILNSEY CRAG

Upper Wharfedale runs from west to east, and contains the villages of Yockenthwaite and Hubberholme with its famous church (the resting place of J.B. Priestly). Miles of drystone walls crisscross the rolling fields, and the spectacular Kilnsey Crag presides over the valley and attracts climbers and walkers alike.

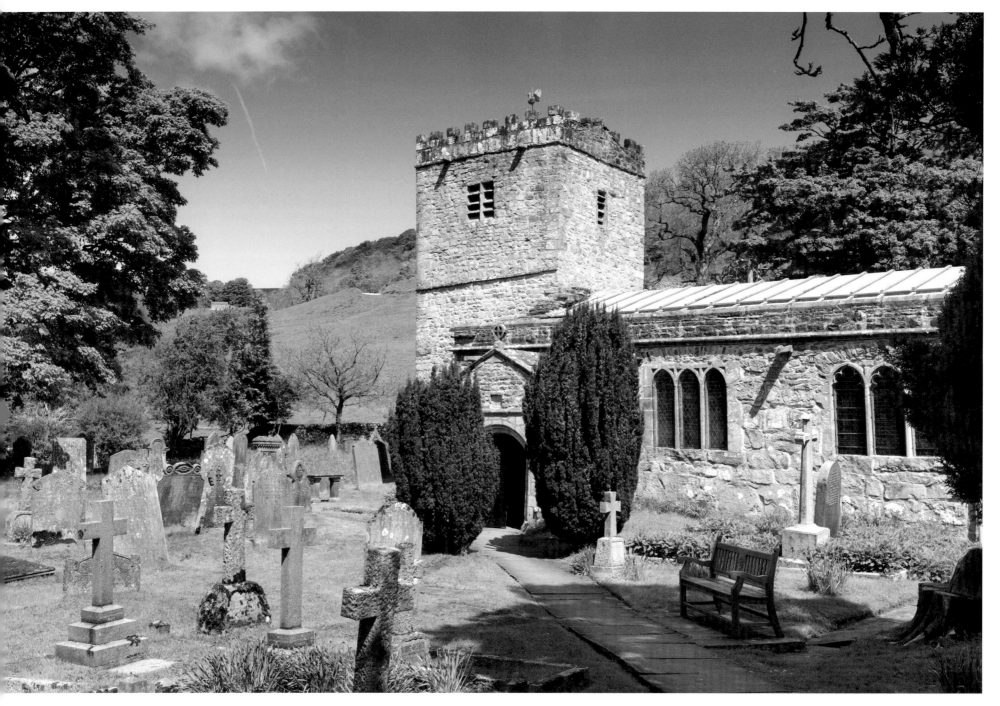

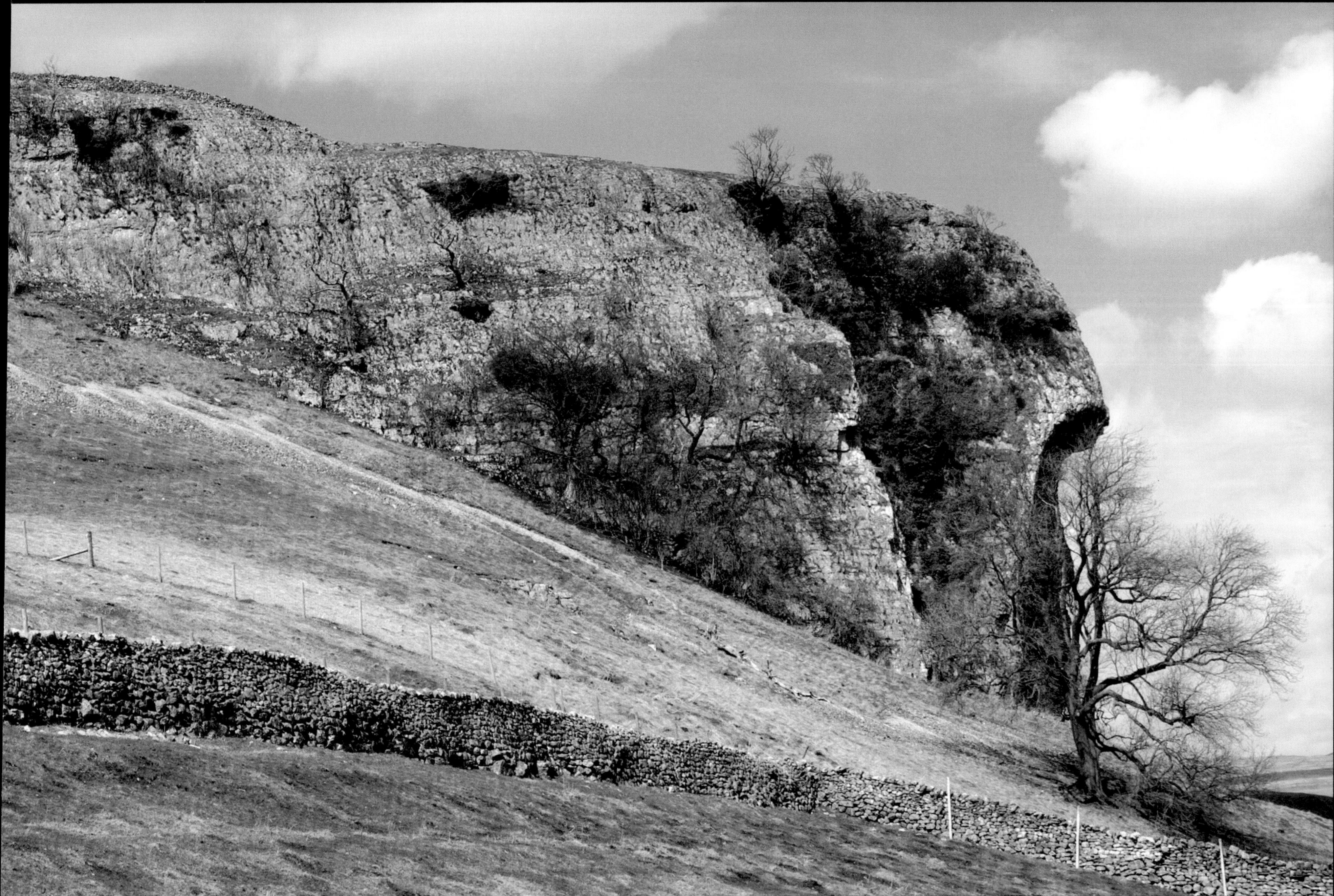

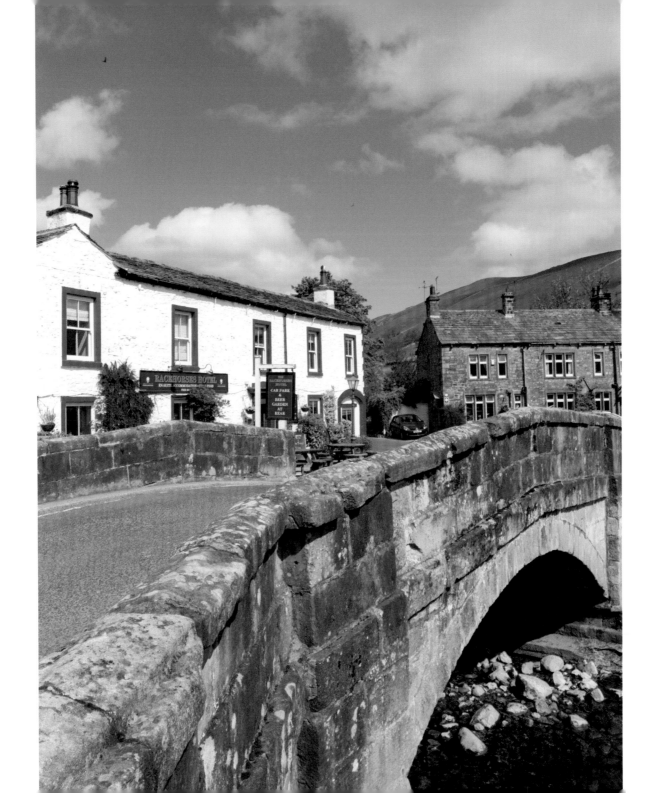

LOWER WHARFEDALE

WATERFALLS, BRIDGES AND STEPPING STONES AT LINTON

Limestone gives way to gritstone as Wharfedale proceeds south and east past Grassington, providing a contrast between the lead mining heritage of the gritstone uplands and the agriculturally productive limestone field systems. Ilkley Moor, with the famous Cow and Calf Rocks, attracts many tourists, most of whom know the unofficial Yorkshire anthem – *On Ilkley Moor Bah't 'At!*

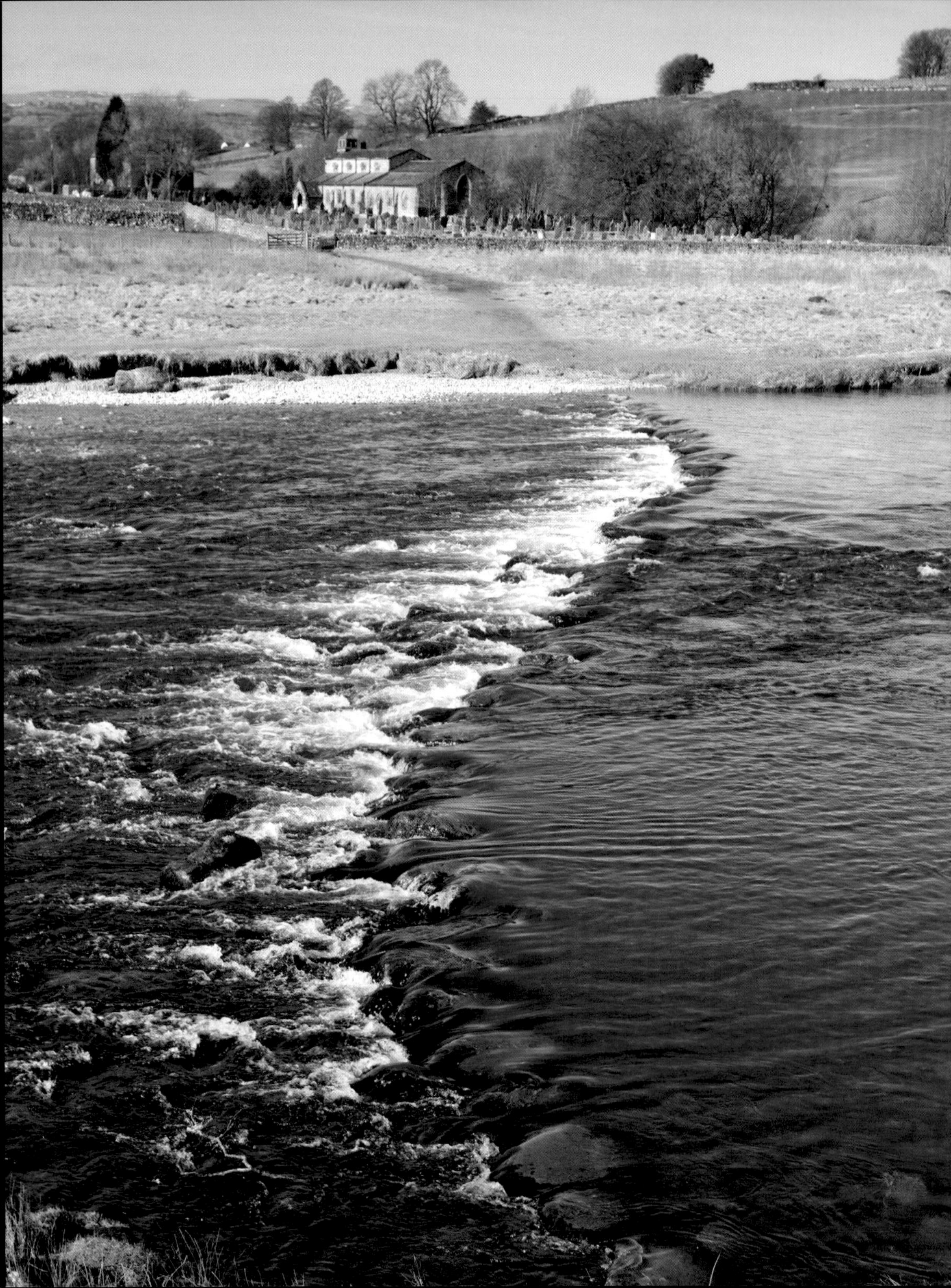

NIDDERDALE

MIDDLESMOOR AND
GOUTHWAITE RESERVOIR

Nidderdale deserves its status as an Area of Outstanding Natural Beauty. The River Nidd flows through underground caves for part of its upper course, rising at Nidd Head, near Lofthouse on the slopes of Great Whernside, and feeding the Angram, Scar House and Gouthwaite reservoirs before joining the River Ouse in the Vale of York.

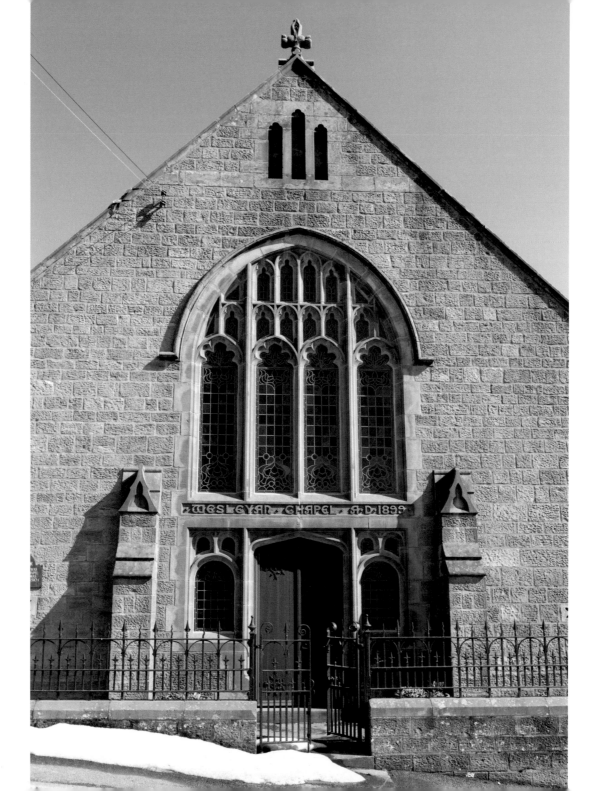

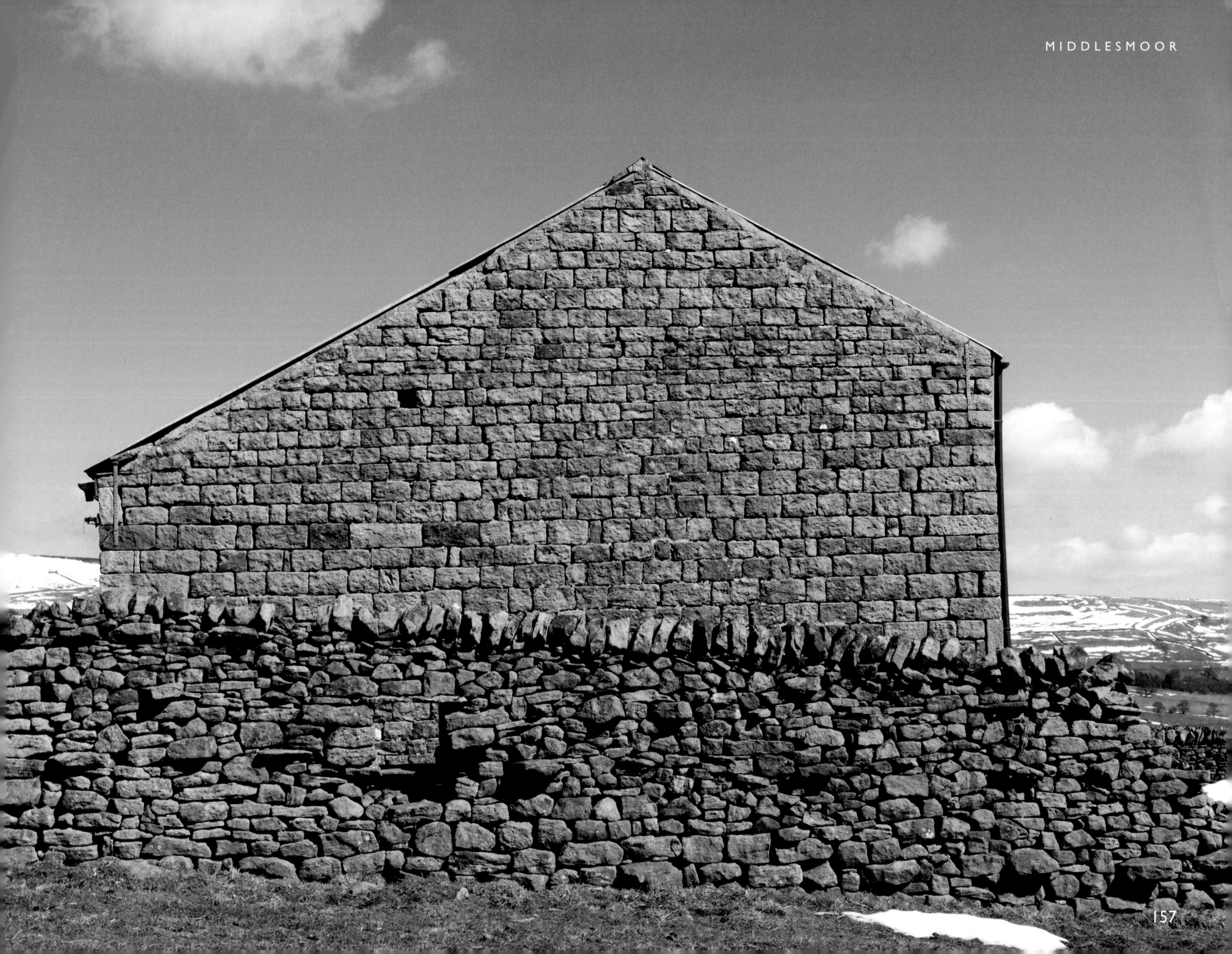

UNTIL NEXT TIME...

Our photography has taken us on a journey that has been both challenging and rewarding. There have been lows, when we have struggled with the elements and our equipment and wondered if all the effort would be worth it, but these have been far outweighed by the soaring highs of seeing our images on screen and in print.

Our first publication on the Peak District allowed us to share our love of our local area, and with this book we have enjoyed being able to expand our horizons and bring you some of our images from the beautiful Yorkshire Dales. Our only regret is that there are so many stunning places in Yorkshire that we simply could not fit them all within these pages! We have a vast portfolio of images from many different areas, and we look forward to sharing more of them with you in future books.

Andrew & Susan Caffrey